The Whole Works

Careers in Publishing and Printing

Author
    Eleanor Felder

Photography
    Robert L. Miller

 **RAINTREE EDITIONS**

Library of Congress Number: 75-5903

Printed in the United States of America

Published by Raintree Editions

 A Division of Raintree
Publishers Limited
Milwaukee, Wisconsin 53203.

Distributed by Childrens Press
1224 West Van Buren Street
Chicago, Illinois 60607

Library of Congress Cataloging in Publication Data

Felder, Eleanor.
    The whole works: Careers in Publishing and Printing

    SUMMARY: Discusses the various jobs and processes involved in making a book and their interrelationships.

    1. Printing, Practical—Vocational guidance—Juvenile literature. 2. Publishers and publishing—Vocational guidance—Juvenile literature.
    [1. Printing, Practical—Vocational guidance. 2. Publishers and publishing—Vocational guidance. 3. Vocational guidance] I. Miller, Robert L. II. Title.
    Z243.A2F36   686.2'2   76-5903
    ISBN 0-8172-0700-7
    ISBN 0-8172-0701-5 lib. bdg.

1☐2☐3☐4☐5☐6☐7☐8☐9☐0☐   80☐79☐78☐77☐76☐

Contents

1	The Whole Works	5
2	The Publisher	7
3	The Author	10
4	The Editor	13
5	The Designer	16
6	The Photographer and Illustrator	19
7	The Typesetter	22
8	The Paste-Up Artist	25
9	The Printing Plant	27
	Estimator	
	Photographer	
	Stripper	
	Platemaker	
	Press Operator	
10	The Bindery	34
11	The Shipper	39
12	The Bookseller and Librarian	41
	Glossary	

For Sam and Leon

1

The Whole Works

There are printed things around us all the time. A cereal box. A movie ticket. A candy wrapper. A dollar bill. And, newspapers, magazines, and BOOKS.

Who does the printing? What jobs need to be done to turn an idea into a candy wrapper? Or a book? It took the work of many people to turn the idea for this book into the book that you are holding. As you read, you will see how the work was done.

Each job is important to the making of a book. Each worker counts on the others to do their jobs well. All the jobs must be done well for the book to be good.

6

2

The Publisher

Who decided that this book should be printed? And how much money to spend making it? Who thought that you would want to read such a book? Who made it possible by bringing together a writer with an idea, and the people and materials to make a book? The answer is: the PUBLISHER.

A book publisher is the head of a company that produces books. The publisher makes many decisions that guide the company. The publisher decides what kinds of books to print. Stories? Picture books? Dictionaries? What will it be?

The publisher also decides how many different books to print. And, how many copies of each one. The more books printed, the more money spent. If the publisher prints more copies of a book than can be sold, the publisher loses money. If this happens often, the publisher will not be a publisher long.

What other kinds of things does a publisher decide? The date that the book will be finished and ready to sell. The price of the book. The amount of money to be spent on the book.

There are even more money matters. The people who write the book, make the book, ship the book, and sell the book must be paid. The publisher must pay them all, but not spend more money than was planned.

You can see that the publisher must know how to run the business. But a publisher must know more than how to run the company. The publisher must know a good book idea when it comes along. And know people and their reading habits. The publisher brings ideas and people together through books. To do this, a publisher must understand money matters, people, and books.

3

The Author

Publishers need books to print. And writing books is the job of writers or AUTHORS. Sometimes an author has an idea and suggests it to the publisher. Or, the author may have an idea, write a book, and send the book to the publisher. Sometimes a publisher gives the author an assignment to write a book on a certain subject. The publisher does this just the way a teacher gives a student an assignment to write a report.

The writer might be asked to think up an idea for a story, make it into a book, and have the book finished in six months. Sometimes the book is fiction, a story that comes from the writer's imagination. Sometimes the book is nonfiction, writing that is based on facts or true information. If the author does not have the information needed for the book, a trip to the library is in order. Authors may have to do a lot of homework or research before beginning a book. They look up facts in books at libraries and museums. They talk to experts, people who know a lot about a subject. And, they go on field trips to see for themselves.

Once all the facts are gathered, the writer must organize them. Often writers make an outline, or list of all the things they want to say in the book. The author follows the outline when writing. Having an outline helps in organizing the book. And keeps the author from forgetting ideas or information.

Next comes the writing. Authors try to write clearly so that people will understand what they are saying. And they try to make the book interesting so the reader will finish it. Often the author must work hard to finish a book by the time it was promised. If the writer is late finishing the book, everyone else who works on it may be late also. Then the book might not be ready at the time the publisher had agreed. People who have heard about the book and want to buy it might be angry at having to wait. They might buy a different book instead.

Writers often are asked where they get their ideas. Writers sometimes get ideas for stories from things they hear or see or read. A writer might see a newspaper picture of a lizard. The picture gives the writer an idea for a story about a monster that looks like a giant lizard. Or, an author might be visiting a museum. There the author sees a mask and gets an idea for a story about the person who wore the mask. Or, for a book explaining how masks were made. Or, for a story about a make-believe animal having a body to go with the mask.

A writer might read about a girl living alone on an island. The writer begins to imagine the adventures she might have had. How did she live? What did she eat? What happened to her? And the next thing you know, a story is born.

4

The Editor

A publishing company may have several EDITORS. An editor reads an author's work and decides if it is clear and correct. The editor reads the work very carefully. Over. And over. And over again. One time, the editor reads for the story or idea. Another time, to be sure that the spelling and punctuation are right. After changes have been made, the editor reads the work again.

The editor always finds something to say about the manuscript. Manuscript is the word for the text of a book that has not been published. If a manuscript is good, the editor praises it. If a manuscript is partly good and partly bad, the editor points out the bad parts. If a manuscript is all bad, the editor sends it back.

Like a teacher, an editor writes notes and questions. The editor may say that something does not make sense. Or, ask why some word was used. The author may be asked to write some parts over. The editor works with the author to make sure that the book is as good as it possibly can be.

An editor does other things also. An editor may

suggest books that the company might publish. If the publisher likes the editor's ideas, the editor finds an author to write the book.

When the author is found, an agreement, or contract is made. The author agrees to write the book, usually by a certain date. The publisher agrees to pay the author a certain amount of money. The editor keeps track of the contracts. And makes sure that all the promises are kept.

Each day's mail brings manuscripts that writers send. The writers hope that some editor will like their work. Another part of the editor's job is to read these manuscripts that come without anyone's asking.

Sometimes the editor is helped by a MANUSCRIPT READER. The manuscript reader reads all the manuscripts that come to the publisher. The best ones are then chosen for the editor to read. Many manuscripts will never be published. Some are boring. Or too long. Or on subjects few people care about. The editor and manuscript reader talk over the manuscripts and make a decision.

Besides working on the words for a book, the editor works on the pictures or illustrations. Are pictures needed to help explain the story? If so, what kind of pictures? Photos, or drawings? Who should take the photographs or do the drawings? The editor thinks over these questions. And then tries to get the best possible pictures for the manuscript.

At last the editor thinks that the manuscript is good. The pictures are settled. And the work is ready for the next person who will help it become a book.

5

The Designer

The DESIGNER plans how the book will look. Before planning, the designer must know something about the book. What kind of a book is it? A picture book with few words? A book with mostly words and few pictures? Who will read the book? Children? Adults? The designer tries to imagine people looking at the book. What will make them want to read it?

Often, the first thing people notice about a book is the cover. The designer must be sure that the cover attracts attention. And makes people want to look at the book.

How does the designer begin? One thing the designer must know right away is the amount of money the publisher plans to spend on a book. Knowing how much money there is for a book helps in deciding such things as the number of pictures to use. And the kind of paper. Designers have to think about costs all the while they are planning a book.

The designer and the editor choose an artist or a photographer for the book. Together they plan pictures that will suit the book.

The way the words look must suit the book also. The designer decides how big the print should be. Often books for young people have print the size of the print in this book. If the print had been bigger, you might have thought the book looked babyish. If the print had been smaller, you might have thought that the book was too hard for you to read. While planning the print size, our designer imagined you looking at the book. And wanting to read it.

But it is hard just to imagine how the pages will look. The designer needs to see how they will look. Needs to see if the pictures and words fit together. Needs to see if there is enough room for everything.

And so a layout is made. A layout shows where the words will go on a page. And where the pictures will be. The layout is made on a piece of paper the size of the real pages. The designer looks at the layout. Do the pages look the way the designer had imagined? Do all the words and pictures fit? The designer would not want to come to the last page and have too many words to fit on it. Or, to have a picture left and no room for it. A layout helps designers make sure that their plans will work.

Many book designers have studied art. Some are artists themselves. A book designer needs a good imagination. The designer must be able to work with many different kinds of books. And make each one exciting. Just as the editor senses when a word is right, the designer senses when colors are right. And spaces. And sizes. And the way the pages look. The designer takes the writer's ideas and gives them a shape. In this way, the designer helps to bring together a writer and a reader.

6

The Photographer and Illustrator

Pictures are one of the first things you look at in a book. Pictures may make the story more clear. Or, they may make the book beautiful. Or exciting. Like writing, pictures may come from the imagination. They may show things that never happened. And animals that don't exist. Or, pictures may show something real. Either way, the pictures must fit the text or story.

The pictures for a book may be drawings. The person who draws them is called an ARTIST or ILLUSTRATOR. Pictures in a book may be photographs. The person who takes them is called a PHOTOGRAPHER. An artist and a photographer make pictures in different ways. And with different tools. But they both do the most important thing. They both use pictures to tell you something about the story or give you a feeling about it.

The editor and designer decide what kind of artwork best fits a book. This book is about real jobs done by real people. And so, the editor and designer decided to have a photographer take the pictures.

Many people have cameras and take pictures.

A photographer takes pictures to earn a living. The designer and editor told the photographer what kind of pictures they wanted for this book. The photographer took the pictures and sold them to the publisher. And now you see them in the book.

A photographer must be able to imagine how a picture should look. Then the photographer has to have the skill to take the picture that was imagined.

7

The Typesetter

Before a book is printed, a paste-up of each page is made. Earlier, the designer made a layout to show where the text and pictures should go. The layout just shows lines for text. The paste-up uses the real words. For the paste-up, the text is pasted on a sheet of cardboard the size of the page. An outline showing size and shape is drawn where the pictures will go.

The book page will look just like the paste-up. So the paste-up must be exactly right. Each line must be exactly the right length. There must be exactly the right number of lines on each page. A special copy of the manuscript is made for the paste-up. This special copy is called a proof. The process of copying the manuscript to make the proof is called typesetting.

There are several ways of typesetting. In the picture you see phototypesetting. The TYPESETTER sits at a machine that is like a special typewriter. The typesetter types, or keyboards, the manuscript on the machine. You can see the words that have been typed showing on the screen above the keyboard. The typesetter can check the screen and see if there are mistakes. But, this machine does not make the proof. It makes a tape with holes. The holes on the tape are a kind of code for all the letters. The tape is taken from the typesetting machine. Then it is put in another machine. This machine reads the code on the tape. It copies the words from the tape onto paper. This is the proof used to paste-up the pages.

Another way of typesetting is often seen. This way is called the linotype process. The typesetter types on a keyboard like the phototype keyboard. But when the keys are pressed, metal letters are made. The letters are lined up into words. The words are lined up into sentences. The sentences are made into lines. Then the lines are coated with ink, and a paper proof is printed.

What does it take to be a typesetter? You should be a good speller. And quick with your hands. You have to be able to concentrate. You have to be willing to work carefully and correct mistakes. It takes patience and skill to set type correctly. Word after word. Page after page.

8

The Paste-up Artist

The typesetter checks the proof for mistakes. The proof is then sent back to the editor. The editor also checks it for mistakes. If there are mistakes, they must be corrected by the typesetter. If there are no mistakes, the proof is ready for the PASTE-UP ARTIST. The paste-up artist makes the paste-ups described earlier. A paste-up artist must be very exact. If the text is not pasted down straight, the lines in the book will be crooked. The outline of the picture must be the right size and in the right place. Otherwise, when the real picture is used, it might cover some words. Or run off the side of the page. The paste-up artist must also have patience. And like using a ruler and straight edge.

9

The Printing Plant

The first person met at the printing plant could be the ESTIMATOR. The estimator figures how much it will cost to print the manuscript. The designer tells the estimator the size of the book. Also the number of pages and pictures. The designer also tells the estimator what sort of paper to use. And the number of books to print.

The estimator thinks about all the costs of printing the book. How much paper will be needed? How much ink? How long will it take the people working at the plant to do the work? The estimator figures the costs very carefully. Being right is

important. An estimator must be willing to pay attention to details. And like solving problems. And 28 working with numbers. An estimator takes pride in knowing that the price is right.

If the publisher also thinks that the estimator's price is right, the printer gets the job.

At the plant, the work is given first to the CAMERA PERSON. The camera person photographs the paste-ups. First, films are made of the text. Then separate films are made of the pictures. The films will later be used to make the printing plate.

The camera person has to be sure that the film of a color picture looks like the real picture. Where

there is blue on the original picture, there should be the same color of blue on the film. The camera person must have a good eye for color. And the patience to keep checking until the film is right.

When the films are ready, they are passed on to the STRIPPER. The stripper puts together the film of the text and the film of the pictures. The films are taped down so that the pages look just the way they do in the paste-ups. Each film must be taped in just the right place. The film can't be even a hair's width out of place. Otherwise, the whole page will look crooked.

When the strippers have all the pages ready, they lay them out in rows. Pages are not printed one at a time on separate pieces of paper the way you see them in a book. The pages are laid out side by side in several rows. A whole group of pages is printed on one large sheet of paper. The stripper arranges the pages so that they can be printed on the large sheet.

To be a stripper, you need skill with your hands. You need to be patient. And willing to take the time to measure very carefully. The job needs close attention every step of the way. Strippers take great pains with the job. And, great pride in neat work.

From the stripper, the films go to the PLATEMAKER. The films must be copied onto plates, smooth flat sheets used for printing. If the pictures are in color, the colors must be copied onto the plates. The platemaker must be sure that the colors look the same on the plates as they do in the films.

A platemaker takes pride in making clear, sharp plates. And plates that have the right colors. Good plates make it possible to do good printing.

Now it is the PRESS OPERATOR'S turn to work on the book. Press operators run the printing press. Often there are several press operators running one press. One fastens the metal plate in its place on the press. Another fills the ink holders. An operator loads the press with huge stacks of paper. Then the press is turned on.

Once the press is started, the operators watch for trouble. Many things can go wrong. The paper may jam. Or tear. Or wrinkle. Or, one color of ink may run out.

Even more things can go wrong. Sometimes the powdery chemical used to dry the ink on the sheets does not work. Then the sheets stick together as they are stacked up in the finished pile. To spot problems early, one of the operators reaches into the machine every few minutes. A sheet is pulled out. The operator checks the sheet to be sure that everything is right. Sometimes the operator finds a spot on the sheet. The spot is called a hickey. The hickey is made when a little bit of dirt gets on the roller of the press. Then the operator rushes over and wipes the roller with a rag. Afterwards, another

sheet is checked to be sure the hickey is gone. You can see that press operators have to be alert. They must be able to figure out what is wrong. And fix it. Quickly.

At the end of a job, the press operators wash the ink from the press. They make sure that the press is left in good shape, ready for the next run.

The people who work on a press day after day become a team. They take satisfaction in running their press well. From their training and experience, they understand their machine. They know how to keep the presses rolling.

10

The Bindery

After the sheets are printed, they go to the BINDERY. The bindery is the place where the sheets are folded, fastened together, trimmed, and put inside covers. Some printing plants have their own binderies. Often books are sent to a separate bindery.

The first step in binding is the FOLDING process. This means folding the large printed sheets into pages. An operator feeds a pile of sheets into a folding machine. The machine folds each sheet into a book section.

The three sections that make this book were then put together. This process is called GATHERING. Gathering is usually done by a machine with mechanical arms. As the machine gathers, someone checks to see that the sections are being put in the right order.

When the sections are gathered, they are joined. For some books, the sections are glued together. Other books are sewn. Or spiral-bound like a notebook. The sections in this book were sewn together.

Remember that the sheets were folded into pages. The pages had creases, or folds, instead of edges. After the sections are attached, they are cut on three edges. This is done so that you can turn the pages. The cutting process is called TRIMMING. It is done by a three-knife trimming machine. The operator of a paper trimming machine must be alert at all times. The blade that cuts the paper will also cut a finger. Or an arm. Or whatever is in the way when the blade comes down. Modern machines have safety features that are supposed to protect the operator. But mistakes can happen. The trimmer operator must always keep an eye on the machine. And the position of fingers, hands, and arms.

The next step in bookbinding is placing the book body in its cover. The cover is printed ahead of time. The cover on this book is made of paper treated with plastic. It is mounted on strong cardboard to make it stiff.

After the cover is mounted on board, the front and back pages of the book are glued to the insides of the cover. Sometimes the end pages are made of a special strong paper that will hold the book to the cover. The glue is spread on the front and back pages of the book by a machine. Then the book is placed in the cover so that the front and back pages are glued to the insides of the cover.

Next the operator takes the book and places it into another machine. This machine forms the hinges of the book. The machine also presses out any air bubbles that may have formed under the end pages.

After the books are covered, they are

packed into cartons. Or, wrapped in plastic film or brown paper.

The books are then shipped either to the publisher's warehouse or to bookstores and libraries. Now the binder's job is finished.

11

The Shipper

The book is now ready to go out into the world. How does it get there?

The SHIPPING MANAGER sends out the books. The shipping manager may be at the bindery or at the publisher's warehouse. Books are ordered by booksellers. And by libraries. And by schools. The shipping manager sees to it that people get the books that they ordered.

The books are packed in cartons. Workers check orders carefully to make sure that the right books are in the right boxes. The shipping manager checks to be sure that orders are handled quickly and correctly.

40

12

The Bookseller and Librarian

And now comes the big test. Will people buy the book? Will bookstores, schools, and libraries want the book? Will all the thousands of copies of the book be sold?

The publisher nervously waits to see the sales figures. The author drops by the bookstore to see if anyone is buying the book. The editor watches for good reviews of the book. The designer hopes the book will win a book prize. The book makers use the book to show customers what good work they do. The shipper gets ready for a flood of new orders. And the bookseller unlocks the bookstore door and waits for the buyers.

How do booksellers hear of books? How do they get them? Most booksellers read book reviews. A book review is a description of a book. It tells what a book is about. And whether it is good. Or bad. Most booksellers read the magazines that tell about books. There are even books about books. And lists. Lists of best sellers. Lists of new books. Books for children. Books for adults. Art books. Sports books. Books on jobs. Booksellers watch the lists very closely. They want to have the books that many people want to buy. And sometimes someone asks for a book. A little later someone else may ask for the same book. Soon the telephone rings and another person asks if the bookstore has the book. The bookseller quickly decides to order the book.

The publisher's book salespeople go around to bookstores, also. They show the bookstore owner books from their publishers. They describe books and try to interest the owner or book buyer in ordering some. The book buyers think of the reviews. And the lists. And their own feelings about the book. They

think of the people who come into the bookstore.
Would many of the people want to buy the book? If so,
the bookstore orders the book.

What happens if the publisher was wrong? And
the editor? And the bookseller? What happens if people
do not buy the book? Sometimes books do not sell.
Perhaps the book costs too much money. Maybe the
publisher just printed too many copies. Anyway, people
are not buying the book. The bookseller may send all
the unsold copies back to the publisher. Perhaps the
publisher and bookseller will decide to have a book
sale. The books are sold at a lower price. But they
are sold.

What happens if the publisher was right? And the editor? And the bookseller? Many people want the book. The publishing company and the bookseller earn money. Everyone is satisfied.

Sometimes people want to read a book. But they don't want to buy it. Then they go to the library. How does the library get the book? People who buy books for libraries read the book reviews, too. And the magazines. And the lists. The LIBRARIAN thinks about the book. Will it interest people? Will it help people to learn? Is it a good book that people will want to read? If so, the librarian orders the book for the library.

Not all librarians are at public libraries. Some work in schools. But the school librarian asks the same questions. And more. Will teachers have students do reports on the subject of the book? Will the book help students with their work? Will teachers ask students to read the book? If the school librarian thinks that the book would be helpful for students, the school buys it. And once again, the publisher is successful. And the author. And the illustrator. And all the people who worked to make the book good.

And now my work is done. An idea has been turned into a book. The book is in your hands. The people who made the book are proud of it. They hope that it has helped you to understand them and their work.

Glossary

These words are explained the way they are used in this book.

Assignment—a task that you are asked to do

Author—a person who writes a book

Book Review—a description telling what a book is about and judging whether the book is good or bad

Bookseller—a person who sells books

Concentrate—to pay attention

Designer—a person who plans how a book should look

Editor—a person who works with an author to make a book as good as possible

Estimator—a person who figures out how much it will cost to print a book

Hickey—a spot on the printed sheet

Illustration—artwork

Illustrator—a person who does artwork for a book

Librarian—a person who chooses and buys materials for a library and helps readers find books they will enjoy

Linotype—a typesetting process giving lines of metal type used to make a proof

Manuscript—the text of a book that has not been published

Operator—a person who runs a machine

Original Picture—the picture you start with

Paste-up Artist—a person who makes a copy of the page the way it will be in the book

Photographer—a person who takes pictures

Phototypesetting—a typesetting process producing coded tapes from which a proof is made

Platemaker—a person who makes a printing plate

Press Operator—a person who runs a printing press

Process—a special way of making or doing something

Produce—to make

Proof—manuscript that has been typeset

Shipping Manager—a person who sees to it that books are sent out

Stripper—a person who makes a page copy using films of the text and pictures

Text—the words in a book

Typesetter—a person who changes the manuscript into proof form

Typesetting—the process of getting the manuscript in proof form

We wish to thank Lake Book Bindery, Inc., Neyler Color-Lith Co., Inc., and Milwaukee Area Technical College for their cooperation in the preparation of this book.

Westermann Design